RIVERSIDE MUSEUM

A Souvenir Guide

RIVERSIDE MUSEUM

A Souvenir Guide

Riverside Museum: A Souvenir Guide

First published in 2011 by Glasgow Museums. Reprinted, revised and updated in 2014 and 2018.

ISBN 978-0-902752-98-6

Authors:
Jo Anthony, Martin Bellamy, Lisa Brown, Colin Campbell, Scott Coyne, Kirsty Devine, Lawrence Fitzgerald, Alastair Gunning, Tom Ingrey-Counter, Bob James, Jennifer Kinloch, Brian Longworth, Emily Malcolm, Crawford McGugan, John Menzies, John Messner, Mark O'Neill, Anne Reid, Alex Robertson, Heather Robertson, David Scott, Emma Semple, Aileen Strachan, Neil Symington, Kate Tansley, Stewart Thompson, Rosemary Watt, Richard Williams

Edited by Fiona MacLeod
Designed by Alasdair Robertson

Photography supplied by Glasgow Museums' photographers and Photo Library. Freelance photography supplied by Iona Shepherd.
www.ionashepherd.com

www.glasgowmuseums.com
www.glasgowlife.org.uk

Printed in Scotland by J Thomson Colour Printers

Acknowledgements
All efforts have been made to trace copyright holders but if any have been inadvertently omitted, please notify the publishers. The publishers gratefully acknowledge the following for permission to reproduce illustrations:
Mr George Parsonage, p53.

About this book
Of the 1.4 million objects in Glasgow Museums' care, several thousand are on display in the Riverside Museum. As we cannot include every object, in this souvenir guide you will find highlights from the displays, arranged by theme.

The objects were chosen for many different reasons – because they are unique, have an interesting story to tell, are most often asked about, or are representative of a whole group of objects in the collection. Many different people have contributed to this book, and this is reflected in the different styles of writing.

As with all other museums and galleries, sometimes objects are on loan, displayed in other venues, being conserved, or are co-owned, so we cannot guarantee that every object in this book will be on show when you visit. If you are interested in finding out more about any of Glasgow's collections, you can visit Glasgow Museums Resource Centre, in the south of Glasgow or search our Collections Navigator: **http://collections.glasgowmuseums.com**

We hope this book will give you a taste of the Riverside Museum, and look forward to welcoming you again – and again.

CONTENTS

Lord Provost's
WELCOME

Glasgow is proud of having the biggest group of civic museums, and the largest number of museum visits by local people, in the UK. On behalf of the people and City of Glasgow, I am delighted to welcome you, and invite you to share our heritage and contemporary art, which attract 2.4 million tourist visitors each year.

Our network of museums was built in two phases. The first involved the culmination of the great Victorian municipal museum movement, with the People's Palace (1898) and Kelvingrove Museum and Art Gallery (1901), both of which were refurbished in recent years to equip them for the 21st century. The second phase began in 1983, with the Burrell Collection, followed by Scotland Street School Museum (1990), St Mungo Museum of Religious Life and Art (1993), and the Gallery of Modern Art (1996). Glasgow has also invested more than any other city in the UK in providing state-of-the-art storage for its historic collections, in the Glasgow Museums Resource Centre (2004 and 2009).

The Museum of Transport was founded in 1963 to mark the end of the city's trams and after a move to the Kelvin Hall in 1987 it has finally moved to an outstanding building which both preserves the collection and communicates the spirit of innovation and energy which is so much part of Glasgow's past, present and future.

Glasgow is delighted and excited to have an iconic building by an architect of the calibre of Zaha Hadid gracing its skyline and helping to bring the River Clyde back to life. With SS *Glenlee*, which is looked after by our partners in the Clyde Maritime Trust, we offer this wonderful new museum to our fellow citizens and to the world. We hope visitors will find it an inspiring experience which deepens their understanding of Glasgow's and Scotland's role in the world.

Bob Winter
LORD PROVOST

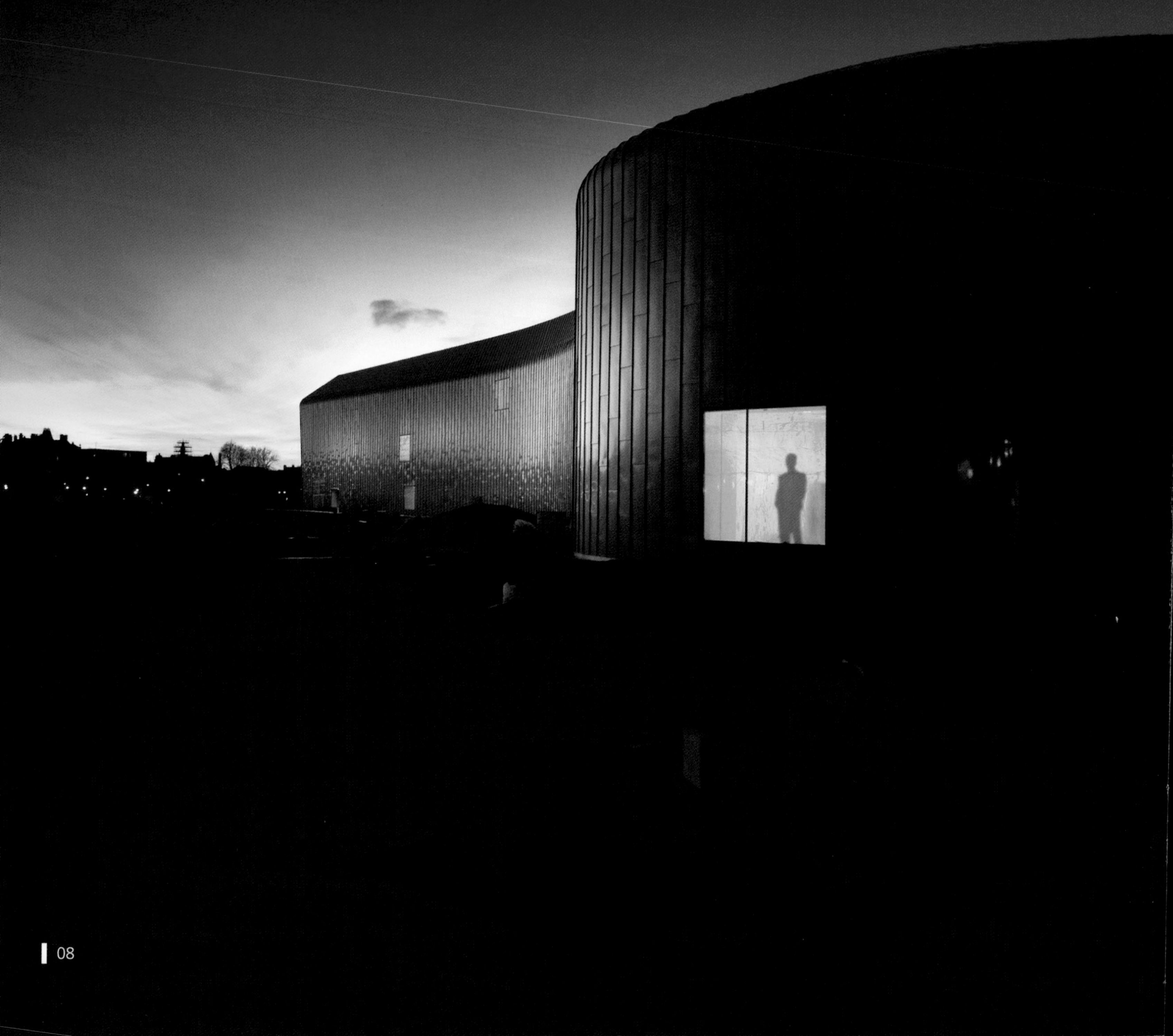

PREFACE

Like generations of Glaswegians, I have always taken great pride in the city's rich cultural treasures, which we enjoy and share with visitors to Glasgow. My personal favourite is the Museum of Transport. From its original home in the Tramway Sheds in the southside of Glasgow, to the Kelvin Hall, the Museum of Transport has always been a much loved Glasgow institution.

In the early summer of 2011 the Museum of Transport moved to its new home – the Riverside Museum, an innovative and breathtaking landmark building on the banks of the Rivers Clyde and Kelvin, designed by leading architect Zaha Hadid CBE. I hope you will enjoy the experience of visiting the museum and appreciate how the building dramatically re-presents the collection of objects that we know and love.

Supporting the creation of this stunning new museum, the Riverside Museum Appeal had many highlights – from initial launch, to bringing the South African Locomotive 3007 to George Square in August 2007, to securing major commitments from FirstGroup, BAE Systems, Weir Group and Arnold Clark, amongst others, and hosting a successful Gala Dinner at Riverside on 25 March 2011.

The task of the Appeal was a challenging one given the prevailing economic climate. However, good progress was made and we will always be grateful for the support of companies, trusts and more than 3,000 individuals who helped this cause and added their support to the creation of Riverside.

Lord Smith of Kelvin
CHAIRMAN, RIVERSIDE MUSEUM APPEAL

Riverside Museum –

A NEW ERA
ON THE CLYDE

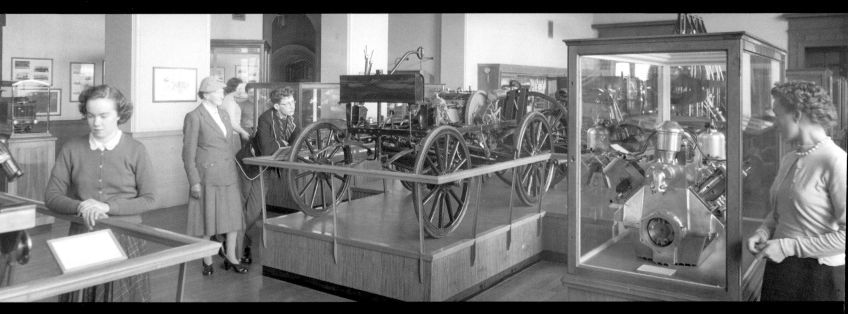

The Engineering Gallery at Kelvingrove, 1958.

The Riverside Museum is the new home for Glasgow's world famous transport and technology collections. The origins of the collection date back to the 1860s when Glasgow was a thriving industrial city earning a reputation as the workshop of the world and the second city of the Empire. In order to provide a shop window for its engineering talent and to inspire and educate its citizens the City Industrial Museum was opened in 1870 in Kelvingrove Park. Here you could find engines, models and samples from Glasgow's important chemical, textile, locomotive and shipbuilding firms.

As additional exhibits were added the museum quickly became over-crowded, and by the 1880s the city decided to build an impressive modern museum that would reflect the growing ambitions of Glasgow. The result was Kelvingrove Art Gallery and Museum, opened in 1901. Its famous ship model court and engineering gallery inspired generations of budding young engineers and transport enthusiasts.

Meanwhile Glasgow had created one of the finest public transport systems in the world. A first-rate collection of important trams and other vehicles was preserved, but it was not until the tramway system closed down in 1962 that an opportunity came to create a new museum. The trams were joined by a number of locomotives, buses, horse-drawn vehicles, cars and fire engines at the old tram depot at Albert Drive to create Glasgow's first Museum of Transport in 1964. With one of the best transport and technology collections in the country displayed in an atmospheric workshop setting it proved to be a great success.

Kelvingrove, with Kelvin Hall to the right, 1955.

In 1976 the ship models moved from Kelvingrove to create a 'Clyde Room' at Albert Drive. However, despite its popularity, the tram depot was never designed to house a museum and it was difficult to maintain the exhibits in good condition. When the Kelvin Hall was redeveloped in the 1980s it provided an ideal opportunity to create a new museum of transport, which opened in 1987.

During the 1980s and 1990s Glasgow successfully re-invented itself as a city of culture. The Clyde began a process of transformation from dirty backwater passing through semi-derelict industrial badlands into a focus for urban renewal. The Clyde Waterfront regeneration project is rapidly transforming the river into a world-class waterfront with business, residential and cultural amenities. Riverside Museum is a key part of this redevelopment and its riverfront location has also provided a brand new home for the historic *Glenlee* sailing ship.

The City Industrial Museum

The Queen Mother opening the Museum of Transport, 1964.

The museum has been built on an appropriately historic location at the mouth of the River Kelvin. Pointhouse was the site of a crossing to the ancient settlement of Govan. Its rural setting began to change when a small shipyard was established in 1840. This was taken over by A. & J. Inglis who gradually expanded over the whole area. Many fine ships were launched from the yard, including the paddle steamer *Waverley* in 1946.

The site has now given birth to the stunning new Riverside Museum which launches Glasgow's transport collection firmly into the 21st century.

CROSSING THE WORLD

Transport has linked Glasgow with other ports and cities and countries all over the world.

From the 19th to the mid-20th century, Glasgow was a major producer of ships and steam locomotives, responding to the demand to link people and goods with the many parts of the British Empire and the rest of the world. Over 20,000 Glasgow-built steam locomotives were exported to dozens of countries as trains provided the easiest and cheapest way to connect large numbers of people and goods by land. Glasgow and Clyde-built sailing and steam ships enabled millions of people both globally and within Scotland to find and make new homes, flee repression or discover different cultures. Today airports and air corridors and roads have largely overtaken rail as the major carrier of both people and goods across land.

Helen Denny

Figurehead from the *Helen Denny*, 1866

137 cm x 60 cm x 73 cm

Donated by M. & J. Allan, Glasgow, 1964

T.1964.11

Built in Glasgow in 1866, the *Helen Denny* sailing ship made 24 voyages to New Zealand from 1872 until 1896, carrying emigrants and cargo. John Moultray, from Edinburgh, emigrated to New Zealand in 1883 with his parents and brother. His three sisters had died of tuberculosis and the family hoped for a new start in a different country. John kept a diary of their three-month long voyage on the *Helen Denny* in which he described the sunsets, storms and seasickness – and his first impressions of the family's new home in New Zealand.

QE2

Museum display model (based on the original test tank model) of the *QE2*, c.1967

Built in 1979 in the workshops of the Museum of Transport on the original tank testing hull

135 cm x 550 cm x 75 cm

Donated by Vickers Shipbuilding, 1976

T.1976.56

The 1967 launch of *Queen Elizabeth 2* – the *QE2* – was a very special event for Clydebank and Glasgow. Most people suspected she would be the last great liner to be built on the Clyde – and they were right. *QE2* crossed the Atlantic and cruised around the world until 2009. However, she was not just used for pleasure – during the 1982 Falklands conflict she was requisitioned to act as a troop ship.

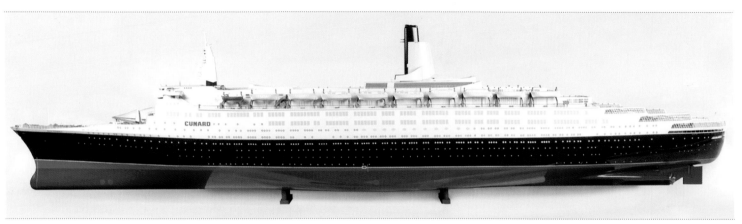

Queen Mary

Builder's model of the RMS *Queen Mary*, c.1930–3

Made by John Brown and Co. Ltd, Clydebank

136 cm x 550 cm x 67 cm; 258 kg

Donated by John Brown & Co. Shipbuilders, Clydebank, 1962

T.1962.6.d

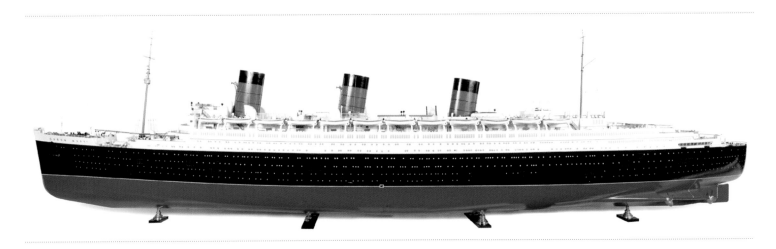

This model of the *Queen Mary* was originally made to test the planned design of her superstructure in a wind tunnel. Her builders, John Brown & Co. Ltd of Clydebank, needed to check that smoke from her funnels would not blow across the promenade decks. They knew that first class passengers would complain if they got soot on their clothes!

The *Queen Mary* was launched in 1934 and made her maiden voyage on 27 May 1936. She was operated by the Cunard White Star Line and was popular with both economy and luxury passengers on the North Atlantic route until her retiral in 1967. Over 1,000 crew were needed to look after more than 2,000 passengers.

South African Locomotive

SPONSORED BY

FirstGroup plc

Class 15F steam locomotive,
1944–5

Made by the North British Locomotive Company at Queen's Park Works, Polmadie, Glasgow

3.95 m x 22.5 m x 3.04 m;
179 tons/182,583 kg

Bought with the support of the National Lottery through the Heritage Lottery Fund, 2006

T.2008.1

This powerful and reliable locomotive hauled passenger and freight trains in harsh conditions across South Africa for 43 years. It was one of over 20,000 Glasgow-built steam locomotives exported to dozens of countries across the globe. In 1948 the all-white government of South Africa imposed a racist regime called apartheid which was applied to all forms of transport. Black people were forced to use separate carriages, ticket offices, platforms, and waiting rooms. A black person could not have driven or repaired this locomotive as all skilled jobs in the South African Railways were reserved exclusively for whites.

TRANSPORT AND LEISURE

We use transport for leisure and enjoyment, to take part in sport or to escape from the city.

Most transport has been designed or adapted for leisure or speed – whether shoes or skis, cars or canoes. The allure of speed has been the driver of records and record holders and Scotland has had more than its fair share of world champions. Transport also supports leisure, which in turn supports transport. Which came first – the wagon, taxi, car, tram, train or the dancehall, football ground, cinema and holiday?

'We may produce better boats Sir Thomas, but we don't produce better men',

early 20th century

By Robert Carter (1874–1918)

Cartoon, tinted ink drawing on paper; 53 cm x 45 cm

Bequeathed by Sir Thomas Lipton 1932.29.ej

Uncle Sam - We may produce better boats Sir Thomas, but we don't produce better men.

Yachting Grocer

***The Gamest Loser* trophy,**

1930

Made by Tiffany of New York, USA

Gold, silver, enamel

44.4 cm x 29.5 cm; diameter 22.5 cm

Bequeathed by Sir Thomas Lipton 1932.29.aj

Glaswegian Sir Thomas Lipton was an ambitious man. By the 1890s, having built up his hugely successful grocery and tea empire, he needed a new challenge. He set his sights on the ultimate prize in international yacht-racing – the America's Cup. In 1930, after his fifth – and final – failed attempt to wrest the America's Cup from the USA, Lipton was presented with this trophy by the American people as a '…symbol of a voluntary outpouring of Love, Admiration and Esteem …to the Gamest Loser in the World of Sport.'

The Flying Scotsman

Racing bicycles, 2004

Replicas built by Graeme Obree

1 m x 1.62 m x 42 cm; 12 kg

Bought by Glasgow Museums, 2007

T.2008.24.1-2

These two bicycles were made for the 2006 film *The Flying
Scotsman*, the story of Scottish sporting hero Graeme Obree's life
and achievements. They are exact replicas of the innovative bikes
designed and made by Obree on which, in the mid 1990s, he achieved
worldwide fame when he broke the world hour cycling record and won
international championships. The handles demonstrate both cycling
positions that Obree was famous for – the 'crouch and tuck' or 'downhill
skier', and 'Superman'.

Board Games

Flyer Bowlrider skateboard, c.1978

Made by Morris Vulcan Ltd, Solihull, UK

11.2 cm x 73 cm x 17.2 cm

Donated by RS McColl Ltd, 1983

T.1983.22

When the Californian craze of sidewalk-surfing – skateboarding – hit the
UK in the late 1970s, no-one imagined how massively popular it would
become. In Glasgow the Council even built a skate rink in Kelvingrove
Park. National competitions were held there where expert skaters like
Glasgow's Jamie Blair showed off their moves in the notorious Jaws Bowl
and the Bazooka Run. Today, fashions and styles have changed
but the tricks, and sense of freedom and identity all remain.

Tram Dancing

Cunarder tramcar No 1392, 1952
4.88 m x 10.74 m x 2.25 m; 16 tons/16,256 kg
Donated by the Museum of British Transport
T.1972.33

In the 1950s Glasgow was 'Dance Hall City', with lots of dance halls to take your pick from. Going to the dancing was what you did at the weekend. Dolled up in your fashionable best, you went to attract the opposite sex or just enjoy an evening's dancing. Trams were a really reliable way to get to the dance hall – and you could meet up with all your pals along the route.

George Pinkerton: rhubarb farmer, speedway racer, Spitfire pilot

Douglas Dirt-track Special Motorbike, 1929
Made by Douglas, Bristol
93.4 cm x 20.8 cm x 80.5 cm; 188 kg
Lent by Margot Allison
LT.1978.53

This is the top-of-the-range Douglas Special motorbike raced by George Pinkerton at White City Stadium, home to Glasgow's speedway craze. It has no brakes or mudguards – they would only slow you down! During World War II Pinkerton – rhubarb farmer, speedway racer and Spitfire pilot – commanded a daring fighter unit. By 1945 George Pinkerton was a decorated war hero with the Distinguished Flying Cross and Officer of the Order of the British Empire.

GETTING THERE

People have experienced obstacles and unexpected ups and downs whilst travelling around Glasgow and Scotland.

Prior to the late 20th century and transport i.e. such as the AC three wheeler car or the accessible Metrocab taxi getting around independently was very difficult for mobility impaired people. The sheer remoteness from the main Scottish cities and the ruggedness of the landscape made travel to and from Scotland's west highlands and islands difficult before the West Highland railway was completed in 1901. Locomotives such as the Glen Douglas or boats such as the Jollyboat were used to connect people and places. During World War I women tram conductors and drivers also played a key role in keeping the trams and people on the move. And what better way for a 1950s' small family to go on holiday than by a Sunbeam motorcycle and side car, especially as the price of a new car was the same as a small house!

Accessible Cab

MCW Metrocab Hackney taxi,
1987

Metro Cammell Weymann,
Birmingham

1.95 m x 4.49 m x 2.04 m

Given by James O'Hara, 1998

T.1998.34

This Metrocab is Scotland's first taxi designed to accommodate wheelchair users. There are removable folding ramps which enable a passenger in a wheelchair to get into the taxi and to travel to their destination whilst remaining in their wheelchair. During its 11-year career, this taxi travelled over 700,000 miles in and around Glasgow. Passengers thought the interior spacious, and described the taxi as looking futuristic in appearance.

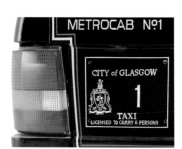

As easy as 1, 2, 3

Dove Therapy Cycle, 1993

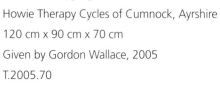

Howie Therapy Cycles of Cumnock, Ayrshire

120 cm x 90 cm x 70 cm

Given by Gordon Wallace, 2005

T.2005.70

Although a rare sight in the UK, people all over the world ride tricycles for many reasons – work, shopping, commuting, sightseeing and fun. This tricycle was adapted for Graham who had just started at a school for children with autism. Graham and his friend cycled around their village on their tricycles. Graham's mother thought the tricycles gave the boys a sense of freedom and achievement, but to Graham it was just his bike.

The Great Tram Gamble

Standard tram 779, 1914

6.2 m x 2.1 m x 9.2 m; 14 ton/14,224 kg

Donated by Corporation of Glasgow Transport Department, 1964

T.1964.35.c

Below right:
Jenny Campbell was a tram conductor and driver.

At the start of World War I Glasgow Tramways had to avert a staffing crisis caused when many of their male employees volunteered for the army. They employed women – as conductresses and even as tram drivers. By the end of the war nearly 2,000 – around one-third – of Glasgow's conductors and drivers were women but they were paid less than their male colleagues. By 1918, the tramways of Aberdeen, Birmingham, Cardiff, Dundee and Edinburgh had followed Glasgow's lead in employing women.

Glen Douglas – the Iron Road to the Western Isles

SPONSORED BY

The Barcapel Foundation

Glen Douglas locomotive and tender, 1913

3.96 m x 17.11 m x 2.7 m; 103 ton/105,515 kg

Donated by the British Railways Board, 1966

T.1966.15.b

The *Glen Douglas* locomotive travelled on the West Highland railway line between Glasgow and Mallaig for over 40 years. Before the completion of the railway in 1901 it would take days by sea or rough roads to reach places like Fort William, the Isle of Skye and the Western Isles. Today, the West Highland Line is thought to be one of the world's most scenic railway journeys.

The Last Tram Procession

Baillie Burt experimental tramcar 1089, 1926

3.8 m x 9.98 m x 2.25 m;
16 ton/16,256 kg

Donated by Glasgow Corporation Transport, 1964

T.1964.35.i

On 4 September 1962, in torrential rain, about 250,000 people lined the four-mile route through Glasgow to watch the trams running for the last time. The trams had been the stalwarts of travelling around Glasgow for 90 years, and many people were very sad to see them go. Robert Cooper, a Glasgow tram driver for 33 years, had the honour of driving one of the trams in the farewell procession.

***The Last Tram Procession**, 1962

R. H. Wyllie

Oil on board, 64.5 cm x 89 cm x 5 cm

TEMP.2709

Independence Day

AC model 70 three-wheeler, 1971

AC Car Company, Thames Ditton

1.46 m x 2.855 m x 1.36 m; 391 kg

Donated by the Scottish Home and Health Department, 1980

T.1980.23

In this invalid carriage there is just one seat which slid over so the driver could get in from their wheelchair. Having the engine at the back meant that the front of the vehicle was light and unstable. Drivers had to be careful whilst driving as sharp turns or strong winds could tip the trike over! But for many drivers who could not drive standard cars or use public transport, 'Wee Bluey' gave a profound sense of freedom.

Horsing Around

Station bus by Henderson & Co., Glasgow, 1896

2.65 m x 7.17 m x 1.91 m

Given by J. Lawson, 1964

T.1964.23

Cabriolet, c.1910

C.S. Windover & Co. Ltd, London

2.35 m x 3.92 m x 1.75 m

Donated by St Cuthbert's Co-operative Society, 1963

T.1963.14.a

This horse-drawn station bus took holidaymakers into Balfron village from the railway station, two miles away. It was a slow, winding journey. By comparison, only very rich people could afford to own a cabriolet – a two-wheeled carriage for one passenger, pulled by one horse, which could weave through a town's busy streets. Cabriolets could zip round tight corners and dart down narrow lanes, leaving larger carriages – like the station bus – far behind.

A Hold-up on the Road

Pair of blunderbuss pistols,
c.1780–1800
Made by Gourlays, Glasgow
11 cm x 27 cm x 2.5 cm
Given by Mr Charles E. Whitelaw
E.1940.45.n and E.1940.45.o

Pistol, c.1850
Made by James Dougall, Glasgow
13 cm x 24.5 cm x 3.5 cm
Given by J. Whitton, 1951
A.1951.16.ao

Travelling in the late 18th and early 19th centuries was dangerous. Highwaymen lurked on country lanes, footpads in dark city streets, willing to murder you for a few pence or a pair of boots. How would you have protected yourself against these cut-throats? A pocket pistol is easy to carry but you had to shoot at point-blank range – so close you would be staring into your attacker's eyes. Holster pistols are heavier and powerful – just the sight of them could scare your assailant away.

Lifeline to the Isles

Jollyboat of the SS *Dunara Castle*, 1875
Made by Blackwood and Gordon, Paisley, Port Glasgow
85.5 cm x 499 cm x 185.5 cm; 240 kg
Given by Mr Peter Morrison, 1995
A.1995.44

St Kilda – a group of islands in the Atlantic over 41 miles west of the Outer Hebrides – is stormbound for much of the year. Access has always been very difficult so the arrival of the SS *Dunara Castle* was a major event. This rowboat, or jollyboat, was the ship's boat for the SS *Dunara Castle*. It got right into the shore to deliver mail and provisions to the islanders, who then sold birds' eggs and tweed to visitors.

**Sunbeam S7 Motorcycle
and Watsonian Sidecar,** 1954/9

1.434 m x 2.17 m x 1.644 m

Given by Harry Fields

T.1985.22

Beardmore Precision Motorbike, 1922

Metal, plastic, wood, leather

1.09 m x 1.51 m x 2.185 m; 226 kg

T.1962.24.e

Jump In

Sidecars – attached to one side of a motorcycle – were especially
popular from the 1920s to the 1950s as an economical alternative to
passenger cars, which were still too expensive for many people.
A motorcyclist's family could cram themselves and their luggage into the
sidecar and set off. Despite the cramped and noisy conditions, many people
have happy memories of their sidecar adventures.

LOOKS AND FASHION

Our taste and desires, as well as what is considered fashionable at any time, can affect the way transport is designed and styled.

It can also determine whether transport is an economic success, like the 1970s' Chopper bike, or failure, like the Sinclair C5. Most transport comes pre-branded and if we can afford it we can buy into the image of our choice – Rolls Royce, Vauxhall or Toyota, Ducati, Lambretta or Dawes. Cost aside, many of us like to impart something of ourselves or culture onto and into transport. Look at the decorated trucks and buses in Pakistan, the customized motorbikes of the US and UK, the car stickers, furry dice and religious ornaments, or even the graffiti-marked buses, trains and undergrounds found around the world. All are expressions of art and identity.

Wheels of Fortune

**Ford Anglia Deluxe Saloon
105E motor car,** 1967

1.45 m x 3.9 m x 1.5 m; 730 kg

Given by James I. Johnston, 1984

T.1984.6

With its shiny chrome, sleek lines and distinctive fins, the Ford Anglia was the shy cousin of a 1950s American popular design trend – exaggerated styling. By 1959 – when the Anglia first went on sale – rationing had ended and Britain's 'age of affluence' was in full swing. Owning a car became the ultimate status symbol for wealthy families. Cars symbolized progress, the future and the design of other products – TVs, furniture, clothes – copied car design features.

Chopper Crazy

Chopper bicycle Mark II,
1971 or 1972

Made by Raleigh, Nottingham

103 cm x 140 cm x 66.5 cm;
18 kg

Donated by Raleigh via Rattray &
Company, Glasgow, 1972

T.1972.24.1

In the 1970s, British kids went
chopper crazy. Giant saddle,
funky handlebars, big back
wheel – children in Britain had
never seen a bike like the chopper
before. But the chopper's iconic
features were nothing new.
Kids in California had long been
customizing their bikes, and
US cycle companies had been
quick to spot this motorbike-
inspired trend. In the UK,
Raleigh developed the distinctive
chopper, which became Raleigh's
bestselling kids' bike.

Make a Difference

Daihatsu van decorated for Salaam festival, 1997

1.9 m x 3.36 m x 1.65 m; overall (without wing mirrors): 1.45 m

Bought by Glasgow Museums, 1997

T.1997.25

This van's design is inspired by the colourful truck art found in Pakistani cities on everything from horse-drawn carts to lorries and buses – with a Scottish twist. The van took part in Glasgow's 1997 Salaam festival, a celebration of Islamic culture and art, and Pakistani and Glasgow artists decorated it together. The decorations represent the meeting of two cultures, with the Karachi eagle, teapots symbolizing generosity, the artists' self-portraits and even Oor Wullie.

Nowhere to Hide

Ship model of SS *War Drake*,
1918
Made by D. & W. Henderson
Shipbuilders, Glasgow
84.5 cm x 264 cm x 35.1 cm;
5.1 kg
Donated by D. & W. Henderson
Shipbuilders, 1962
T.1962.29.a

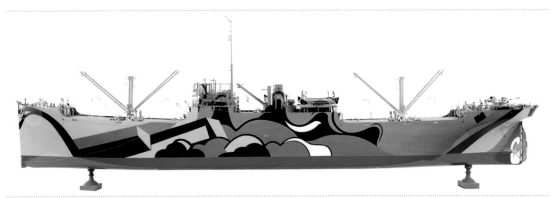

Marine painter, Norman Wilkinson (1878–1971), developed dazzle painting in 1917 to help protect British and Allied ships from attack at sea. Similar to the protective measures evolved by animals and insects, Wilkinson's deceptive and disruptive patterns for ships were designed to cause confusion to enemy submarines. By June 1918, 2,367 Allied ships had been given the 'razzle dazzle' treatment of bizarre, colourful patterns of sloping lines, curves and stripes, in stark contrast to the more traditional colour schemes of ships.

Kolyma Eighty-eight
Catacore kolyma
30 mm x 40 mm x 30 mm
Bought with grant aid from the
National Fund for Acquisitions,
1983
Z.1983.224.537

The Ups and Downs of Clive

Sinclair C5 personal electric powered three-wheeler car with pedal assisted power,
1985
Made by Sinclair Vehicles Ltd, Merthyr Tydfil, Wales
137.5 cm x 172 cm x 70.4 cm
Given by Thomas Sinclair, 1985
T.1986.7

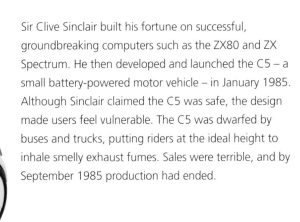

Sir Clive Sinclair built his fortune on successful, groundbreaking computers such as the ZX80 and ZX Spectrum. He then developed and launched the C5 – a small battery-powered motor vehicle – in January 1985. Although Sinclair claimed the C5 was safe, the design made users feel vulnerable. The C5 was dwarfed by buses and trucks, putting riders at the ideal height to inhale smelly exhaust fumes. Sales were terrible, and by September 1985 production had ended.

The Highway (Dress) Code

Argyll Model 6 motor car, 1902

Made by Argyll Motors, Alexandria, Glasgow, Scotland

1.56 m x 3.15 m x 1.42 m

Bought with grant aid from the National Fund for Acquisitions, 1978

T.1978.42

Bentley Sedanca Coupé motor car, 1934

Made by Bentley, England

1.54 m x 4.86 m x 1.74 m

T.1987.38

Today most of us scarcely give a second thought to what we wear whilst driving. But in 1900 the experience of driving was very different – most cars had no doors, roof or windscreen. Occupants sat high up, exposed to the weather, and clothing was your only protection. It took three decades before enclosed cars became commonplace, and by the 1930s only drivers of sports cars continued to wear a cap and goggles – the need for extreme-weather clothing had all but disappeared.

MADE IN SCOTLAND

People in Scotland have applied their ideas, skills and ingenuity to create and construct transport which is used throughout Britain.

Scottish engineers are renowned the world over for their inventiveness and skill. When Gene Roddenberry (creator of 1960s' American TV programme *Star Trek*) was looking for a ship's engineer to keep the spaceship Enterprise fully operational he chose to portray him as a Scotsman. Whilst the prominence of Scottish engineering has undoubtedly declined alongside its manufacturing industry, Scottish engineering inventiveness and skill remains – the systems that power and light the Riverside Museum and the amazing e-labels and audio-visuals that help to bring its collections to life were designed by Scottish engineers.

Caley 123

Caledonian Railway Locomotive No.123, 1886

Made by Neilson & Company, Glasgow

3.94 m x 15.85 m x 2.45 m; 85 ton/86,871 kg

Donated by the British Railways Board, 1966

T.1966.15.a.1

Victorian showpiece, West Coast racer, inspection engine, royal pilot, museum exhibit – this magnificent locomotive started her life as a set of carefully calculated drawings by designers and draughtsmen. Workers then built her in just 66 days – in time for the 1886 Edinburgh International Exhibition. In the 1888 railway races, when rival companies set out to prove which offered the fastest passenger services, Loco 123 was a triumphant winner.

Family Fortunes

Churchill upright coach-built pram, 1968

Made by Churchill Prams, Glasgow

125 cm x 135.5 cm x 59.5 cm; 29.48 kg

Given by Mrs Gallagher, 1992

T.1992.8

Harry Churchill and his son Alf started their Glasgow-based pram business in 1927. Each pram was hand-built using traditional wood, fabric and metal-working skills. By the 1950s, Churchill's was in its prime. Many Glasgow families chose to buy their pram from the company because of its good reputation and local connections. However, Churchill was slow to modernize and competition from larger more innovative pram-making companies led to its closure in 1983.

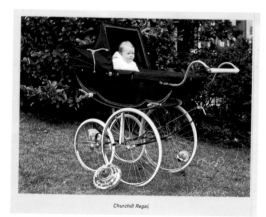

Churchill Regal.

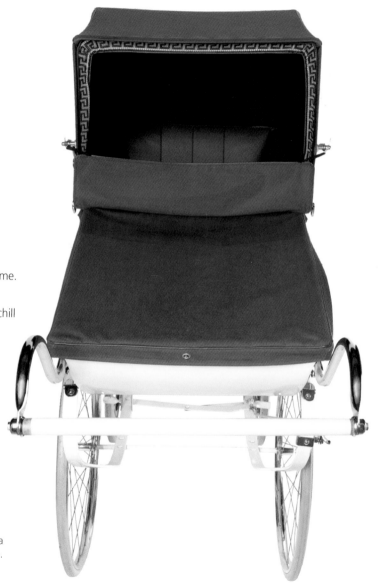

Left:
Photograph from a Churchill brochure.

A Tour of the Imp

Motor car Imp 1, 1963

Made by Hillman Imp, Linwood, Scotland

1.315 m x 3.48 m x 1.47 m

Donated by Talbot (Scotland) Ltd, 1982

T.1982.24

This is one of the first Hillman Imp motor cars off the production line at Linwood in 1963. The Imp is easy to handle and has great all-round visibility. Its distinctive features include an opening rear window with moveable back seats which allow you to turn the Imp into a hatchback – groundbreaking design at the time it was built. It has adjustable front seats and, unusually, the light aluminium engine is set at a 45 degree angle which gives more space for passengers.

The World's Oldest Bicycle...or is it?

Bicycle, c.1846

Built by Gavin Dalzell, Lesmahagow, Lanarkshire

114 cm x 230 cm x 58 cm; 38 kg

Given by Sheriff Blair, c.1909

T.1958.1.a

Gavin Dalzell, a shopkeeper from Lesmahagow in Lanarkshire, built this revolutionary rear-wheel driven pedal bicycle in about 1846. He may have copied an earlier design by Kirkpatrick Macmillan, a blacksmith from Dumfriesshire. It was exhibited at Glasgow's 1888 International Exhibition and the Paris *Exposition Universelle* of 1889, which resulted in posthumous recognition for both Dalzell and Macmillan. Although we are not sure if this is the first ever pedal-driven bicycle, it is the oldest surviving bicycle in the world.

Paisley – Birthplace of the London Cab

Hyper Mark III taxicab, 1932

Made by Beardmore, Paisley

2.09 m x 3.88 m x 1.7 m

Bought with the assistance of the
National Fund for Acquisitions, 2008

T.2008.18

This taxi – designed and built by Beardmore in Paisley – had a long working life of over 20 years in London. A well-designed vehicle and cheap to run, it was as popular with drivers as it was with passengers. Beardmore was a giant Scottish engineering company that employed 42,500 workers at its peak, forging steel and building ships, trains, motorbikes, cars, taxis, aeroplanes and airships.

CUTTING EDGE

PAST, PRESENT, FUTURE

People's desire to travel further, travel faster or travel more safely has pushed designers to be creative in finding solutions.

From the spying helicopters of George Orwell's novel *1984* to Tom Cruise's self-driving car in the film *Minority Report*, transport has long been used as a symbol of the future and cutting edge design and technology. Perhaps that is because for the last 200 years the numbers of ways of travelling and ease of doing so has massively increased and captured the public imagination. Crowds in 1812 must have gawped in amazement at Henry Bell's steam powered ship *Comet* carrying passengers down river from Glasgow twice as fast as anything then known. And in 1895 spectators' reactions probably turned from amusement to incredulity as Glasgow University lecturer Percy Pilcher climbed into and then flew his *Bat* glider.

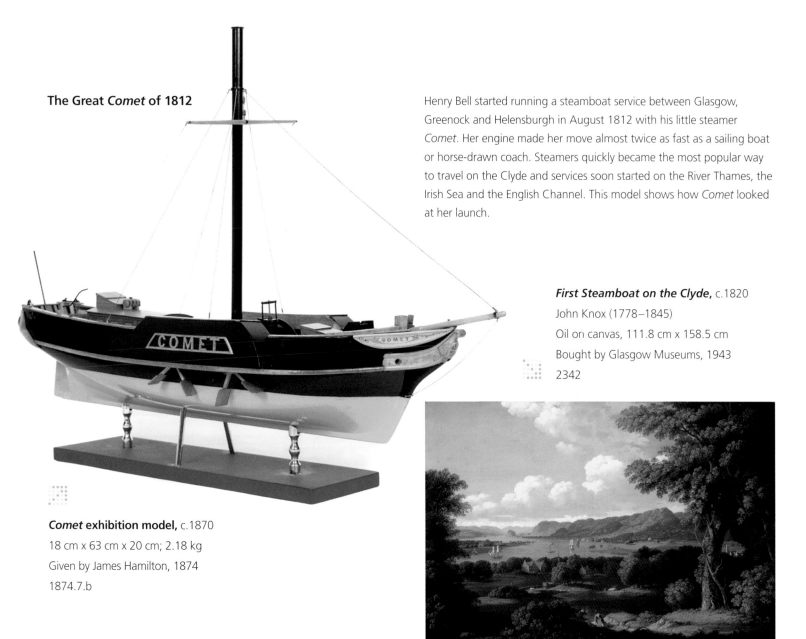

The Great *Comet* of 1812

Henry Bell started running a steamboat service between Glasgow, Greenock and Helensburgh in August 1812 with his little steamer *Comet*. Her engine made her move almost twice as fast as a sailing boat or horse-drawn coach. Steamers quickly became the most popular way to travel on the Clyde and services soon started on the River Thames, the Irish Sea and the English Channel. This model shows how *Comet* looked at her launch.

Comet exhibition model, c.1870
18 cm x 63 cm x 20 cm; 2.18 kg
Given by James Hamilton, 1874
1874.7.b

First Steamboat on the Clyde, c.1820
John Knox (1778–1845)
Oil on canvas, 111.8 cm x 158.5 cm
Bought by Glasgow Museums, 1943
2342

The Legacy of Charlotte Dundas

Forefoot, frame and rail sections of the *Charlotte Dundas*, 1803

Forefoot: overall 27.5 cm x 35.3 cm x 11 cm; 2.2475 kg

Frame section: overall 34.5 cm x 11.5 cm x 9 cm; 1.2475 kg

Rail section: overall: 56 cm x 25 cm x 17 cm; 8.592 kg

Forefoot given by Provost Bogle of Falkirk, 1918

Frame and rail section donated by Thomas B. Seath & Co., 1888

1918.12.a, 1888.48.a and b

Ship model of *Charlotte Dundas*, 1801

32 cm x 59 cm x 17.5 cm; 4.06 kg

Lent by Grangemouth Dockyard Co. Ltd.

LT.1980.38

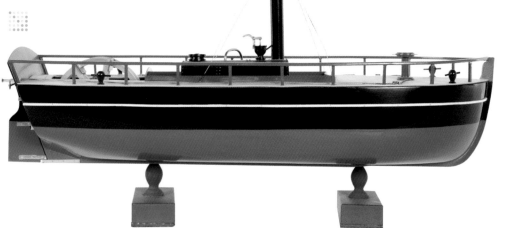

This piece of wood came from the steamboat *Charlotte Dundas*. Engineer William Symington (1764–1831) tested his steamer, his third attempt at building a boat powered by a steam engine, on the Forth and Clyde Canal in March 1803. *Charlotte Dundas* was a success, steaming 20 miles pulling two sailing ships. Symington did not get the chance to develop his ideas further – his main funders pulled out of the project.

The Dream of Flight

Reproduction of the *Bat Mark II*, 2008

Conceived and built by the Pilcher Glider Reproduction Project, Prestwick: David Wilson, Steven Cassells, Ian Adams and Quentin Wilson

2.463 m x 7.315 m x 5.625 m; 25.219 kg

Sponsored by Spirit AeroSystems, British Aerospace and BAE Systems (Aerostructures and Regional), the Clow Group and Autodesk, 2008

T.2008.23

In 1895 Percy Pilcher, a young Glasgow engineer, made his dream of flight come true when he built his own glider, the *Bat*, in his flat in Byres Road. It was exciting and dangerous work – a fall could mean injury or even death. Four years later Pilcher's flying experiments ended in tragedy when he was killed in a crash, aged 32.

DISASTERS AND CRASHES

Transport failure – whether by accident or intent – affects peoples' lives, and the way transport is designed, built and used.

Transport and technology, like life, evolves and changes through failure as much as success. Sabotage and malfunctions have also changed how or even if transport operates. The Gurney steam carriage explosion helped stop steam driven road transport in its tracks and left trains to lead the way. The world's worst shipbuilding disaster, the sinking of the *Daphne* (1883), changed how ships were launched, and the Lockerbie disaster improved airport security – but unfortunately not enough to prevent the events of 9/11. Despite the valiant efforts of rescue services, designers and safety campaigners, death and injury is accepted as a price of transport and travel. A jumbo jet's worth of people are killed on UK roads every month, despite the UK having one of the world's better road safety records.

The Sinking of the *Athenia*

Builder's model of turbine steamship *Athenia*, c.1922

Made by Fairfield Shipbuilding and Engineering Company, Limited, Glasgow

2.463 m x 7.315 m x 5.625 m; 25.219 kg

Lent by the Ballast Trust

LT.1973.12.y

The Donaldson Atlantic liner *Athenia* left Glasgow on 1 September 1939 carrying a large number of children evacuees. Two days later, as she sailed into the Atlantic, Britain declared war on Germany. That night a German U-Boat spotted the liner following a zigzag route with her lights blacked out. The U-Boat captain thought the *Athenia* was a British warship and fired three torpedoes. One struck the liner and exploded. Of the 1,418 people on board, 112 died.

A Crash Course in Safety

Crash-tested BMW Mini Cooper, 2007

1.407 m x 3.699 m x 1.683 m; 1360 kg; overall (wheelbase): 2.467 m

Donated by Euro NCAP, TRL (Transport Research Laboratory) and Thatcham, 2007

T.2007.47

Crash-test experiments are used to see what would happen in car accidents – dummies inside the test car show what both passengers and drivers would experience in a crash. Tests take two weeks to prepare and scientists spend three days afterwards analysing the results. Finally, they give the car a safety rating. This Mini, tested for a head-on collision, scored the maximum five stars for adult occupants and three stars for children in the back.

Shakes and Ladders

Dennis-Merryweather Turntable Ladder Fire Engine, 1940

3.25 m x 9.86 m x 2.3 m

Donated by the Corporation of Glasgow Fire Service, 1966

T.1966.1

For more than 20 years, until the 1960s, Glasgow firemen fought some of the most dangerous fires in the city with this Dennis-Merryweather fire engine. It has a 100-foot long turntable ladder and its centrifugal pump can push out 290 gallons of water every minute. Operating the ladder in co-ordination with the pump required skilled teamwork from the firemen to ensure maximum effect on the fire.

Gurney

Steam drag chassis, 1831

Designed by Sir Goldsworthy Gurney

66.5 cm x 285.5 cm x 206 cm

Given by Professor Pierce A. Simpson, 1889

1889.99

In March 1831 Goldsworthy Gurney (1793–1875) – inventor, surgeon and engineer – made the first ever machine-powered road trip from Edinburgh to Glasgow with his revolutionary steam carriage. Stunned crowds lined the route, gazing at the marvel of the modern age. Just a short while later, on 1 June, his invention was destroyed when, without Gurney's permission, it was started and exploded, injuring two boys. This chassis is all that remains.

The Lockerbie Disaster

Dummy bomb similar to the one used on Pan Am Flight 103

80 mm x 270 mm x 190 mm; 1.396 kg

Given by Dr Jim Swire

T.1998.72.1

The Lockerbie tragedy of 21 December 1988 which caused the loss of 270 lives happened because of security failures. Although terrorist attacks on aircraft are very rare, air travel security is taken extremely seriously throughout the world. Security policy, techniques and equipment are always being updated to meet new threats. In 1990, to demonstrate the need for constant vigilance, Dr Jim Swire (whose daughter died in the Lockerbie atrocity) flew to New York with this homemade dummy bomb to test airport security. Staff failed to find it.

Launch Day Disaster

Photograph of *Daphne*'s salvage taken from Stephen's yard and north bank of the Clyde, 13 July 1883

Henry A. Lewis

Given by Jill Andrews, 2007

T.2007.6.1

Clock presented to John Clink on 23 October 1883, 1883

30 cm x 30 cm x 18 cm

Lent by Mr and Mrs Buick

LI.2006.019.1

The world's worst shipbuilding accident happened on the Clyde on 3 July 1883. A total of 127 men and boys died when SS *Daphne* capsized just after she was launched at Alexander Stephen & Sons' Linthouse shipyard. Stephen's ran its own ambulance service which acted immediately to save lives – the efforts of Henry Clink and the 27 other members were rewarded with the grateful thanks of their colleagues and one of these clocks.

Toucans and Lollipops

School Crossing Patrol uniform

Used by Lollipop Lady, Betty Martin, in her duties outside Elmvale Primary, Springburn, Glasgow, about 2012

'HIGH VIZ WARNING CLOTHING', Fox Wear, Bristol Oilskin & Overall Co. Ltd

PROP.350.1, .2, & .3

School Crossing Patrol Lollipop Sign & Pole

Donated by Mrs Betty Martin & Cordia [Services] LLP, 2016

PROP.350.4

The Lollipop Lady's distinctive uniform of bright fluorescent yellow hooded coat with reflective banding, trousers and cap ensures she is clearly visible in all weathers. She holds her large 'lollipop' STOP sign. School Crossing Patrol workers are celebrated for their crucial role in protecting children crossing the road from the ever-present dangers of road traffic.

THE RIVER CLYDE

Over the centuries, changes to the River Clyde have both powered and reflected developments in Glasgow as it grew from a small riverside hamlet to become a major port and industrial city.

The Clyde is home to wildlife, a means of leisure and a site of trade, travel and tragedy. Dredging the river in the 19th century opened up opportunities for commerce but also helped destroy wildlife. Shipyards once covered its banks supplying ships of all shapes and sizes to the world. Today shipbuilding and port activities are of a different scale, but life and activity is returning in other ways. New businesses, homes and leisure attractions have moved to the river's edge, and along with people and buildings, wildlife has returned.

Rescue on the River

Bennie, c.1954–2010
Glasgow Humane Society lifeboat
4.42 m x 1.385 m; 170 kg
Given by George Parsonage of the
Glasgow Humane Society, 2010
T.2010.16

Since 1790, the Glasgow Humane Society has been based at Glasgow Green – its mission to prevent accidents and to rescue people from the city's rivers. In 1954, Ben Parsonage BEM (1903–79), Officer of the GHS, designed and hand-built the *Bennie* wooden rowing boat for rescuing people and recovering bodies from the River Clyde. *Bennie*'s shape and strength gave her great stability, and her unique design features meant Ben or his son George could haul a body into the boat safely and easily.

Blockade Runners: Glasgow's Role in the American Civil War

The *Ad-Vance* was one of dozens of Glasgow-built paddle steamers sold during the American Civil War to Southern rebel forces to run the naval blockade of their ports by Northern ships. These fast, shallow draft ships took armaments and other supplies into harbours such as Wilmington and Charleston and brought out cargoes of cotton sold to raise money for the Confederate army. Vast profits and huge risks were associated with this secretive trade.

These vessels commanded a high price and the city of Glasgow profited greatly from their sale and construction. However, there was opposition in the city to this involvement with the Southern States where slavery was still legal – slavery had been banned in the British Empire from 1833.

Blockade runner *Ad-Vance*,
about 1864
By Samuel Walters
Oil on canvas; 65 cm x 96 cm
Donated by George Porteous Scott, 1917
1917.24.c

Robert Napier – the Father of Clyde Shipbuilding

Builder's half hull ship model of HMS *Black Prince*

52 cm x 288 cm x 19.9 cm; 46.98 kg

Lent by Wm Beardmore & Co.

LT.1.1931.e

Robert Napier is hailed as the 'father of Clyde Shipbuilding'. A great engineer, Napier was constantly searching for ways to improve the design and building of engines and ships. Napier knew that people were as important to success as machines – he valued his staff, trained them well and rewarded their ideas. Many of his foremen went on to start their own shipyards, which gave Napier a personal connection with most of the shipyards on the Clyde.

Anchor Line

Glasgow's Anchor Line produced beautiful posters in the 1920s and 1930s to advertise their sailing routes around the world. Colourful and romantic images were designed to appeal to the imagination and our sense of adventure. This magnificent elephant decked in gold, feathers and tassels seems about to step right out of this poster advertising Anchor Line routes to the east. A jolly image of a woman in nautical themed clothes gives the impression of a carefree holiday at sea.

Anchor Line to Gibraltar, Egypt and India

Poster, 1926

Gordon Nicoll

Given by Anchor Line, 1982

T.1982.2.34

Anchor Line Cruises

Poster, 1935

Given by Anchor Line, 1982

T.1982.2.45

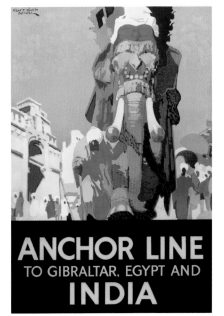

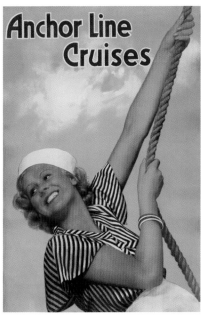

Upper reaches of the Clyde near Elvanfoot.

The Clyde estuary, mudflats at Ardmore Point.

From Source to Sea

The Clyde provides a wealth of habitats for wildlife. Its estuary supports large numbers of overwintering wildfowl and waders, including an internationally important population of redshanks. They are attracted by the rich feeding available on the mudflats. The freshwater habitats of the upper river are home to different species such as otters, kingfishers, dippers and brown trout. Recent improvements in water quality mean that salmon can migrate up the river, as they did before industrialization polluted the waterway.

Redshank
Tringa totanus
170 mm x 270 mm x 90 mm
Z.1982.221.85

Otter
Lutra lutra
233 mm x 709 mm x 313 mm
Gifted by Stephen Munn, 2010
Z.2010.22

HIGHLIGHTS!

HIGHLIGHTS

Ship Cases and Ship Conveyor

SPONSORED BY

The Hugh Fraser Foundation

Builder's model of river steamer *Nepaul*, c.1909

40cm x 220cm x 49cm; 33.72 kg

Donated by William Denny & Brothers Ltd

T.1956.10.i

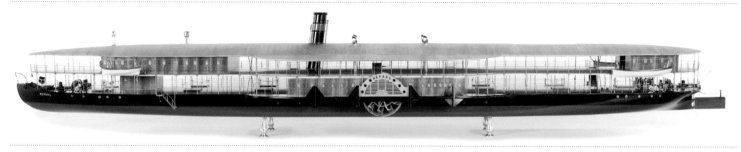

One of the glories of the collections, the ship models are celebrated in three displays on both floors. On the Ship Conveyor you can follow the stories of the vessels and marvel at how these Clyde-built ships served the world. On the main floor our two wall displays reveal some more stars of the collections, and upstairs you can learn why ship models were made.

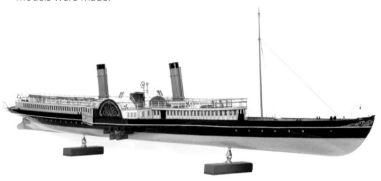

Exhibition model of PS *Iona II*,
1863

47 cm x 27 cm x 165 cm

Donated by Garvel Shipyard, 1963

T.1963.3

**Amateur model of puffer
Northlight,** c.1960s

47.5 cm x 76 cm x 42.5 cm

Given by Mrs Taylor, 2004

T.2004.133

Ship Launch Show

Very few of us have the opportunity today to experience being at a ship launch. Ships are still launched on the River Clyde and it remains an enthralling and overwhelming experience for the viewer. Learn how the complicated launch process happens and experience something of the scale and excitement of being there.

Launch flag from Clyde Marine Motoring,
c.20th century

118 cm x 188 cm x 16 mm

Given by Hamish Munro, 2006

T.2006.43

HIGHLIGHTS

Shoes and Mobility

Walking is our basic mode of transport – but our feet need protection. They need to be kept warm, cool and the soles of our feet and toes need help to cope with rough and uneven surfaces. Shoes can be used to give messages, specialist shoes have been developed for many different activities, like climbing or dancing ... and we choose shoes also just for decoration and fun.

Manfield man's boots, c.1975–85

Given by Miss Govan, 1991

23cm x 9 cm x 27cm

E.1991.43.a and b

Baby's shoes, c.19th century

4 cm x 11 cm x 5.3 cm

Given by Dr Dudgeon, 1877

1877.141.ab.1 and 2

Baxter 'Star Special' Roadster, 1936

98 cm x 176.5 cm x 47 cm; 12kg

Given by Mr William Sanderson, 1994

T.1994.84

The Infinite Velodrome

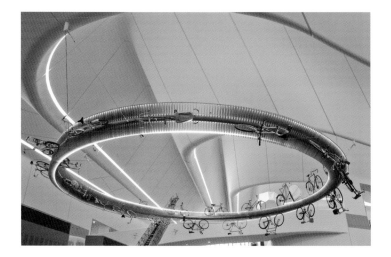

So many very different bicycles whizz around the velodrome. Take a tour of all the bikes with the Scottish cycling legend, Graeme Obree. See some of the adverts that enticed you to invest in a new bike, where you bought bikes like these in Glasgow, and what kind of advice you were given to help you look after your bike.

Dursley-Pedersen Gent's bicycle, 1897–1902

123 cm x 176 cm x 50 cm; 18 kg

Given by David Rattray and Company, Glasgow

T.1961.10

HIGHLIGHTS

Motorcycle Wall

SPONSORED BY

The W M Mann Foundation

Play the motorbike game! Beat your mates – and find out which of these splendid and complicated machines is the fastest, earliest, heaviest, longest; which travelled the further to get to Glasgow, which was driven last, which is the 'greenest', is the most comfortable to ride or has that indefinable 'wow' factor.

Zenith motorcycle, 1913

104 cm x 205 cm x 79 cm; 106 kg

Given by A. E. Watt, 1963

T.1963.2

Triumph Bonneville Silver Jubilee T140J, 1977

106 cm x 223 cm x 74 cm; 186 kg

Given by Mrs Agnes M. MacFarlane, 1986

T.1986.23

Rest and Be Thankful

SPONSORED BY

Glasgow City Council Landfill Communities Fund

The steep gradient and tight hairpin bends of the old Rest and Be Thankful road connecting Inverary and Arrochar are legendary – finally getting to the top was the reason to give thanks! See the types of car which companies tested on the hill, learn about the time trials and the races where top drivers raced up this challenging road against the clock.

The Rest and Be Thankful inside Riverside Museum.

HIGHLIGHTS

The Arnold Clark Car Wall

SPONSORED BY

Arnold Clark Automobiles

Explore every car on display – their interiors and engines. Learn about all the manufacturers, some once very famous for their innovations, but now long gone. Listen to the sounds of the cars and create your own soundscape by layering the car sounds.

Argyll motor car, 1900

1.4 m x 2.01 m x 1.07 m; 580 kg

Given by A. A. Glennie, 1938

T.1938.103

Porsche 911 T sports car, 1980

1.25 m x 4.25 m x 1.76 m; 1315 kg

Given by Mr Silvio Izzi, 2002

T.2002.22

Haldane sports car HD300, 1994

1.22 m x 3.89 m x 1.53 m

Bought with 50% grant aid from the National Fund for Acquisitions, 1997

T.2004.17

No. 9 Locomotive

Find out how the No. 9 Locomotive, built by North British Locomotive Company, Springburn, Glasgow in 1917, was created – from initial design drawings to the completed engine. Learn all about the locomotive's long and unglamorous life as a workhorse, shifting, moving and pulling heavy loads.

Tank locomotive No. 9 of the Glasgow and South Western Railway, 1917

3.53 m x 8.09 m x 2.75 m; 36 ton / 40,641kg

Donated by British Transport Commission, 1966

T.1966.15.e

THE STREETS

CANADA
£2
DALMARNOCK
Drysdale Shoe & Bootmakers
PAWN BROKER
THE MASTER POLISHER
THE MASTER POLISHER
BOOTMAKER
11
543

MAIN STREET

SPONSORED BY

The Gannochy Trust

Cross over the cobbles in Main Street and you'll be in Glasgow of the 1890s to 1930. So much has changed, yet a great deal remains familiar. The Saddler's reminds us of the importance that the horse once had in all our everyday lives, and both the tramcar and hearse are pulled by horses. But we still take our shoes to the cobblers like Mr Drysdale's for repair, where even today very similar machinery is used, and we can jump on the Subway to whisk us home.

Each era has its distinctive 'look'. The dressmaker's – Devine's Gowns and Mantles – is inspired by Murielle's, a fashionable ladies' dress shop from 1910 on Sauchiehall Street. The Cabinet Maker's and Upholsterer's display the stylish furnishings designed, made and sold by Wylie & Lochhead in Glasgow. Head into Ovinius Davis, the Photographer's, to have your picture taken and experience the excitement this new technology brought to ordinary families.

Today, Glasgow abounds with pubs and cafés, and both the Mitre Bar and Le Rendezvous Café use interiors from two real Glasgow venues. In the Anchor Line offices, you could have booked the passage to a new life in Canada or Australia, or the holiday of a lifetime in India or Egypt. The Pawnbroker's reminds us that life was hard for many – work could be elusive and money always short. Often all you could do was pawn your coat or wedding ring, week in and week out.

Bootmakers

PAWN BROKER

THE MASTER
POLISHER

BOOTMAKER

REPAIRS DONE
WHILE YOU WAIT

BS
1511

STREET TWO

STREET THREE

The 1930s to 1960 is the focus for Street 2. The Toy Shop – with its model trains, aircraft, boats, lorries and cars, carpet sweeper, board games, construction sets, tea set and toy yachts to sail on the local pond – shows off many of the toys that every Glasgow child in the early decades of the 20th century wanted to play with.

Murielle's continued to dress well-to-do Glasgow ladies and her tailor-made gowns can be seen in the dress shop window. The technical equipment in the Instrument Maker's window reminds us of the importance that maritime-related industries still played in Glasgow. The Subway was as popular as ever and had been modernized and was driven by electricity.

The Cinema takes us back to the time when Glasgow was 'Cinema City' with 138 picture houses to choose from. Rattray's of Glasgow inspired the Bicycle Shop where we can see just how popular the bicycle had become with both men and women.

Inside the Toy Shop – inspired by the Clyde Model Dockyard in Argyll Arcade – we're surrounded by the train sets, model cars, sailing boats and lorries that were the dream of every small boy.

Street 3 brings us through the 1960s right up to the 1980s. The short hemlines and vibrant colours of the dresses by Glasgow's own Marion Donaldson in the Dress Shop window conjure up the Swinging 60s, as do the organic shapes and strong colours of the Italian-designed plastic furniture on display in the Interior Design Shop.

The need for the services of the Pawn Shop remains, but the goods being pawned have changed and now include novel electronic household items such as a microwave, alongside the usual jewellery and other personal and domestic wares.

Garages have long replaced stables for horses, and the prized family car receives its first MOT, obligatory for all cars 10 years old and over from 1960. Both the Baby Shop and Toy Shop show just how much choice there was by this time for ordinary shoppers, from the prams and knitted woollens for the newest member of the family to the amazing range of children's toys and games, including Star Wars figures, Sindy dolls, Action Man and the first computer games.

THE FUTURE

The Riverside Museum could not have been created without your help. Visitors and users of the old Museum of Transport, local people and tourists have advised us on which collections they prefer, what they want to know about them and how to make the displays and facilities better meet their needs. They have also made invaluable contributions to the displays by donating collections, images, memories and thoughts. We want this to be more than a one-off relationship and conversation.

The displays are designed and laid out to be flexible and easily changed. With the thousands of objects in our care, Glasgow Museums can never display all of the city's collections at once. We welcome your views to help shape the museum in the future. What would you like to see, what stories should be told, what collections are missing?

You can tell us digitally, using the Feedback Stations amongst the displays and seating areas, or fill in an electronic comments card. You can email, write to us or talk to one of the staff. What is important is that Riverside's future belongs to you – help us shape it.

PATRONS

Glasgow City Council and Glasgow Life would like to acknowledge the very generous support given by the Patrons of the Riverside Museum. Through their very significant donations to the Riverside Museum Appeal they have helped create the Riverside Museum as well as providing ongoing partnerships to sustain future activities.

riverside
museum appeal
Celebrating Glasgow's Transport History

Patron	Display Sponsored
BAE Systems	BAE Systems Plaza - External Learning Space
The Gannochy Trust	Main Street
FirstGroup plc	South African Locomotive
The Hugh Fraser Foundation	Ship Conveyor
The Robertson Trust	The Robertson Trust Learning Space
The Weir Group Plc	The Bridge
Arnold Clark Automobiles	The Arnold Clark Car Wall
Glasgow City Council Landfill Communities Fund	The Rest and Be Thankful
The Hunter Foundation	
Optical Express Group	
A J C Smith	
Lord and Lady Smith of Kelvin	
Richard Burns	
Bank of Scotland	Education Packs
Sir Tom and Lady Farmer Foundation	
Strathclyde Partnership for Transport	Subway stations
The Barcapel Foundation	The Glen Douglas
The W M Mann Foundation	Motorcycle Wall
Scottish Hydro	
Alma and Leslie Wolfson Charitable Trust	
Royal Bank of Scotland Group	
Rolls-Royce plc	Education Programme Partnership
Caledonian MacBrayne	Maritime Partnership